OUT ON A LIMB

Riddles about Trees and Plants

by Scott K. Peterson
pictures by Susan Slattery Burke

Lerner Publications Company · Minneapolis

To my Mom and Dad   —S.K.P.

*To my dear parents, Jean and Jim, for their undying
enthusiasm for even the silliest of illustrations   —S.S.B.*

Copyright © 1990 by Lerner Publications Company

This book is available in two editions:
Library binding by Lerner Publications Company
Soft cover by First Avenue Editions
241 First Avenue North
Minneapolis, Minnesota 55401

Library of Congress Cataloging-in-Publication Data

Peterson, Scott K.
    Out on a limb: riddles about trees and plants/by Scott K.
Peterson; pictures by Susan Slattery Burke.

        p.   cm.—(You must be joking)
    Summary: A collection of riddles about trees and other plants,
including "What tree has the most bark? A dogwood."
    ISBN 0-8225-2328-0 (lib. bdg.)
    ISBN 0-8225-9582-6 (pbk.)
    1. Riddles, Juvenile. 2. Trees—Juvenile humor. [1. Trees—Wit
and humor. 2. Plants—Wit and humor. 3. Riddles.]I. Burke,
Susan Slattery, ill. II. Title. III. Series.
PN6371.5.P47   1990
398.6—dc20   89-36629
                                                                CIP
Manufactured in the United States of America   AC

    2   3   4   5   6   7   8   9   10   99   98   97   96   95   94   93   92   91

Q: What flowers live in pickle jars?

A: Daffo-dills.

Q: What is a tree's favorite fruit?
A: Pine-apple.

Q: Why do pine trees buy just ice cream?
A: Because they already have the cones.

Q: What do you get when you cross a barn with a pine tree?
A: A needle in a haystack.

Q: What kind of flowers can you find in zoos?
A: Tiger lilies.

Q: Why did the woodpecker hit her golf ball into the tree?

A: Because she wanted to get a hole in one.

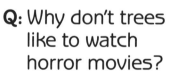

Q: Why don't trees like to watch horror movies?

A: Because they get petrified.

Q: What kind of plant likes gymnastics?
A: A tumbleweed.

Q: How do trees clap?
A: With their palms.

Q: Why didn't the tree play checkers?
A: Because she was a chess-nut.

Q: What flowers talk during April and May?
A: The ones with two lips.

Q: What did one maple tree say to the other?
A: "You sure are a sap."

Q: Why wouldn't anybody talk to the oak tree?
A: Because she was too hard to deal with.

Q: What kind of trees do gypsies read?
A: Palm trees.

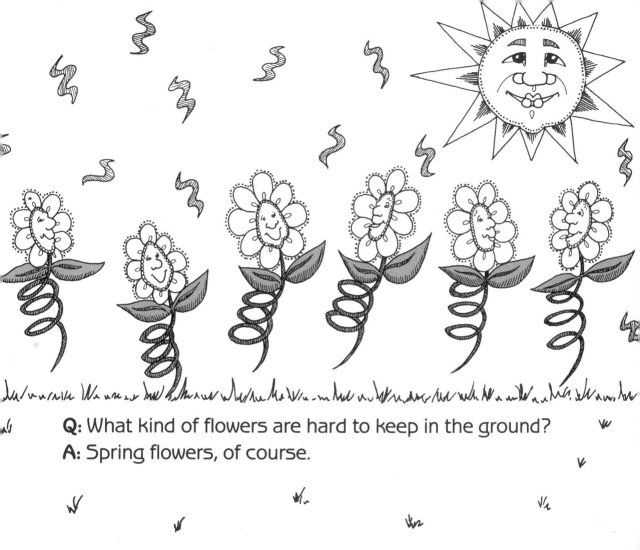

Q: What kind of flowers are hard to keep in the ground?
A: Spring flowers, of course.

Q: Why did the tree go to the dentist?

A: Because she needed a root canal.

Q: Why did the willow tree buy a box of tissues?

A: Because he was always weeping.

Q: What flower has the best eyesight?

A: The iris.

Q: Why don't you ever see trees at the beach?

A: Because they are always forgetting their trunks.

Q: Why was the tree wearing sunglasses and carrying a towel?

A: Because he was a beech tree.

Q: Why are flowers like stores?

A: Because they open in the morning and close at night.

Q: How did the corn plant lose all her money?

A: By playing the stalk market.

Q: Why wouldn't the banker give the tree a loan?

A: Because she didn't want to go out on a limb.

Q: Why did the woman bury all her change in the garden?
A: She wanted to have rich soil for her plants.

Q: Why are trees so successful?
A: Because they are always reaching new heights.

Q: Why did the tree want to be a jeweler?
A: Because he had so many rings.

Q: What kind of coats do trees wear?
A: Douglas Firs.

Q: Why did the twigs go to Washington?

A: Because they wanted to belong to different branches of the government.

Q: Do trees have secretaries?

A: No, they keep their own logs.

Q: Why didn't the hemlock trust the oak tree?

A: Because the oak looked a little shady.

Q: What did Mr. and Mrs. Tree name their son?

A: Woodrow.

Q: Why are vines so lazy?

A: Because all they want to do is hang around.

Q: What did one shrub say to the other shrub?

A: "I think I'll lie down; I'm bushed."

Q: What tree tires easily?

A: A rubber tree.

Q: What happened to the tree who came home late?
A: He was grounded.

Q: Why don't flowers talk?
A: Because it's hard to get them to open up.

Q: Why was the bush always fibbing?
A: Because she was a lie-lac.

Q: Why are acorns so obnoxious?
A: Because they are always acting like nuts.

Q: Why did the plant go on stage?
A: He wanted to be under the lights.

Q: What flower is the king of the garden?
A: The dandy-lion.

Q: What did the Egyptians call their flowers?
A: Mum-mies.

Q: How can you tell if a woman has wild-flowers?
A: If you can see the lady's slippers.

Q: Why can't you find a comb in the jungle?
A: Because there is so much brush.

Q: Why did the tree take a bath?
A: Because she wanted to spruce herself up.

Q: Why are flowers such good friends?
A: Because they started out as buds.

Q: How do trees relax?
A: They get together and shoot the breeze.

Q: Why do trees laugh?
A: Because they tell a lot of oaks.

Q: Why couldn't the trees figure out the riddle?
A: Because they were all stumped.

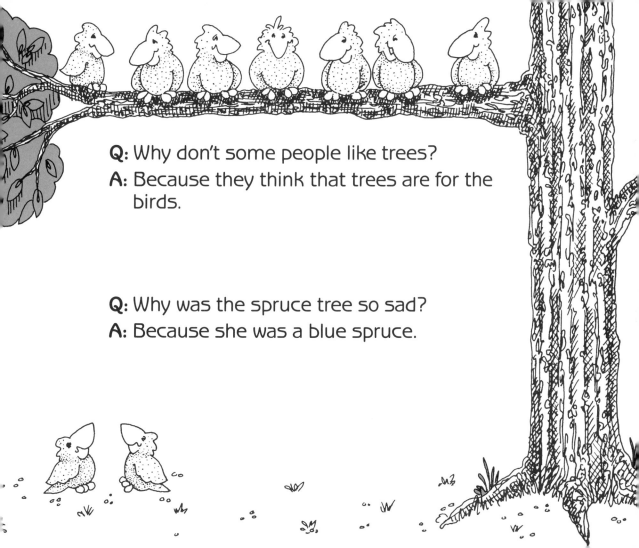

Q: Why don't some people like trees?

A: Because they think that trees are for the birds.

Q: Why was the spruce tree so sad?

A: Because she was a blue spruce.

Q: What did one tree say to the other?
A: I think it's time we split.

Q: How fast can a pine tree travel?
A: About twenty knots.

Q: Why is there always a kitten by the swamp?
A: Because he's looking for his cattails.

Q: What do you get when you cross an evergreen tree with a pig?

A: A porky-pine.

Q: What tree has the most bark?

A: A dogwood.

Q: Where do nice children plant flowers?
A: In a kinder-garden.

Q: How do trees get so smart?
A: They learn from their tree-chers.

Q: How do you measure sod?
A: With a yardstick, of course.

Q: Why did the vine go to college?
A: Because he wanted to join the ivy league.

Q: Why did the teacher put the tree in the corner?

A: Because he was a naughty pine.

Q: How can you tell when two vines are in love?

A: Because they are always clinging to each other.

Q: Why didn't the girl flower go out with the boy flower?

A: Because he never aster.

Q: Why wouldn't the tree settle down in one spot?

A: Because she was made out of driftwood.

Q: Where do trees keep their luggage?

A: In their trunks.

Q: Why did the tree pack her trunk?

A: Because she was leafing town.

ABOUT THE AUTHOR

Scott K. Peterson has always been able to make somebody laugh about something. A graduate of Coon Rapids High School, he has lived in Minnesota all of his life. Scott comes from a family of five brothers and one sister. They all have a great sense of humor, including his mom and dad. Thanks to their help and encouragement over the years, this book is dedicated to them.

ABOUT THE ARTIST

Susan Slattery Burke loves to illustrate fun-loving characters, especially animals. To her, each of them has a personality all its own. Her satisfaction comes when the characters come to life for the reader. Susan lives in Minneapolis, Minnesota, with her husband, her dog, and her cat. She is a graduate of the University of Minnesota. Susan enjoys sculpting, travel, illustrating, entertaining, and being outdoors.

You Must Be Joking

Alphabatty: Riddles from A to Z
Help Wanted: Riddles about Jobs
Here's to Ewe: Riddles about Sheep
Hide and Shriek: Riddles about Ghosts
    and Goblins
Ho Ho Ho! Riddles about Santa Claus
I Toad You So: Riddles about Frogs
    and Toads
On with the Show: Show Me Riddles
Out on a Limb: Riddles about Trees
    and Plants
That's for Shore: Riddles from the Beach
Weather or Not: Riddles for Rain
    and Shine
What's Gnu? Riddles from the Zoo
Wing It! Riddles about Birds